Incongruity

Sheri Banks

BookLeaf Publishing

India | USA | UK

Presentation by *BookLeaf Publishing*

Web: www.bookleafpub.com

E-mail: info@bookleafpub.com

ISBN: 9789357213868

First edition 2022

PREFACE

The poetry within these pages are excerpts of memories and emotions that are relatable. There is no singular theme and is a bit incongruous, but that is the nature of life. These pieces are meant to resonate with readers of various stages in life, as the ideas and emotions have resonated with me. Each may reach you differently, depending upon age, upbringing, or mood. My hope is that you will find something you can connect with in these works.

Summertime

Last school bus ride of the year
Youngsters eager to forget about books and
exams
Lilacs blooming, pinks and purples and blues
Their scent pleasantly pungent
Bees awakening for the season

Lying on the grass, cloud-gazing
With the backdrop of a bright blue sky
Songbirds singing their callings
Clothes on the line soaking up the warm sun
Crisp, clean, fresh

Roses blooming in the soft breeze
Charcoal grill lit and smoldering
Hamburgers and hot dogs cooking
Friends gathered, lounging and eating
Simply enjoying being: present, still, full

Family camping trips at the lake
Fishing for dinner
Casting and waiting
Line taut, the jerk of a pole
Zipping lines and cranking reels

Boats buzzing,
Inner tubes and water skiers zipping behind

Jet skis zooming and darting
Canoes and kayaks sluicing through the water
Children splashing and swimming

Campfires at dusk
Sharing ghost stories and s'mores in the dark
Fireworks explode in the night sky
Sparks showering down to the horizon,
gunpowder in the air
Viewers exclaim their joy with the displays

Fresh rainfall from the previous night
Lingering scent of dampness in the air
Puddles shriveling as the sun travels higher in
the sky
Bicycles appear and roam the neighborhood
Dogs barking, kids shouting

Sunflower fields ablaze in golds
Following the sun as it traverses the sky
Melting temperatures late in the season
Back-to-school shopping deals proclaimed
A steadily escalating sense of foreboding

Lilacs pruned for next year
Rose hips preparing for dormancy
Sunflowers drooping, seeds harvested
Blink and it's over, another season gone
A new one on the horizon

My Heart

I will never understand the phrase
"It's just a dog."
Bringing a pet into my home
To care for and nurture and love
Isn't "just" anything.
Not anymore than I am "just a person."
I wonder, would anyone label me so simply?
A dog is so much more,
Attaching strings to my heart
Perhaps more easily than another human can.
She relies on me for everything -
Food, shelter, medicine, exercise, affection.
And she rewards me with the greatest love I
could ever know.
Sharing her favorite toys with me after my long
day at work;
Zoomies at random moments to burn off energy
and make me laugh;
Head tilts of cuteness when I speak in that voice;
Dance parties in the kitchen that involve singing
and barking;
Cuddles when I am sad from a heartache, no
matter how large or small.
She passes no judgment
And seeks no ill-will.

My happiness is her happiness.
My sadness is her sadness.
She speaks a different language,
But she is more observant than many folks
And she understands me entirely.
We don't give dogs enough credit.
We definitely don't deserve them.
Not "just" a dog…
A best friend.
Family.

Walls

Stones build walls
Around my heart
I've been hurt before
Including by you
These walls are strong.
One letdown is all it takes
A breach of trust
Leads to despair
And heartache.
It's difficult to let someone inside
When I know what disappointment feels like
My faith in humanity is challenged.
Trying to keep my heart safe
Tackling this world on my own
Independence is a badge of honor.
But walls don't discriminate
All souls are kept at arm's length
Including those without fault.
Slow to trust
Quick to block
Free to live on my own terms
Even if I have to do so alone.
Is it really freedom?
Learning to love myself
And take care of myself first

Strong enough on my own
Inside these walls of protection.
I see you
I hear you
Trying to knock down these walls.
I know it's exhausting,
Taxing your strength.
Are you the one with the right tools
To create a window
And join me inside
So we can lean on each other
To keep the world at bay?

Tranquility

Water quietly splashes as it flows by
Current and wind intermingling
I sit on the shore
My favorite place to be.
Listening to the trickling
Fish breaching the surface for food
Leaves softly rustling in the breeze
Abating the hot summer sun.
Dragonflies darting
Birds swooping
And landing in trees on the opposite shore
Even they seem to understand
The tranquility of the afternoon.
A peace overcomes me
As I take in the scenery
This is when I feel closest to God.
His beauty surrounds me
Enveloping me in a calmness
And serenity that fulfills me in this place.
It's why I return here so often
As the season allows
To recharge
To reconnect.
No matter how life is going
This is my safe space
Where I know God is with me
Showing me His beauty
And sharing his love.

Ride or Die

A memory seeps in
An echo in my mind
A fleeting moment lost in time
Why did you have to leave?
Why so soon?
I miss you
Torment

Conversations long gone
Deep into the night
Connection, intrigue
Showing me love is possible
Sharing hopes and dreams
I love you
Warmth

Struggling daily without you
Overwhelming anxiety
Depression, aversion
Fear of asking and sharing
Sinking into cowardice
I hate you
Despair

What is it about love

That can make us feel
Every emotion on the spectrum?
It tears at our hearts
Yet fills them to bursting
I appreciate you
Beloved

Each day is a gift
I struggle to continue accepting
With you not by my side
We are a team
I can't bear this
Without you
Ride or Die

First Love

Read me a story
And hold me tight
Tuck me in
Kiss me goodnight.

I'll be your sidekick
Through thick and thin
Ask you a million questions
Bring you to your wit's end.

Teach me a song
I'll sing all my days
Thinking of you
Whenever it plays.

Never too busy
Or too tired
To be there for me
For all the trials.

Learning by watching
Showing me the way
Taking in life skills
Throughout every day.

Exuding true love,
Kindness, and virtue
So I settle for nothing less
Than what I see in you.

As I've grown older
I've never stopped learning from you
Guiding me in your footsteps
With us, it's nothing new.

I'll always appreciate and love you
We're bound at the soul
Forever and ever
Daddy's little girl.

Runner's High

Cool, crisp morning air
Blackness before sunrise
Complete silence and stillness
No cars
No birds
No people
So quiet it's almost eerie
Set the pace
Jogging down the street
Footsteps keeping the steady beat
Like a pendulum
Breathe in, breathe out
In time with my footsteps
Passing houses that are slowly waking up for the
day
Lights turning on in kitchens
Movement past windows
I press on
Focusing on pace and breathing
Slow and steady
Body loosening
Enjoying the rhythm
Cathartic
Birds awakening as the sky begins to lighten
Stars fading in the grayness
A lone car passes
Muffler rattling

Stereo thumping
It disappears out of site
Silence returns
Only my footsteps and breathing remain
This is my tranquility
Before the chaos of the day can take over
Before my mind starts to race with every task
Simply pacing myself
Taking in my surroundings as the world comes
alive
As I route back toward home
Breakfast smells seep out of windows
My stomach yearns
My heart rate quickens
I increase my speed
Pinks and oranges on the horizon
The sun will make its appearance shortly
Rounding the bend to my driveway
Stopping to catch my breath
And stretch
I take in the scene
Still quiet in the morning light
But more lively than only a short time ago
Birds chirping and fluttering on branches
A dog barking
I take a deep breath
Contentment in the morning glow
I am calm
And ready to conquer the day

Orange

The sunrise as the sun crests the horizon
Soft hues intermingling in the early sky.
Crisp fall weather
Maple leaves changing
And pumpkins for Halloween.
Flowers - so many flowers -
Marigolds and tiger lilies in the summer
Chrysanthemum blooms in the fall.
Monarch butterflies and orioles
Flying in the backyard.
Mangoes and cantaloupe -
Summer fruits!
Squash and carrots -
Fall vegetables!
Fish - so many fish -
Goldfish, starfish,
Clownfish - Nemo!
Fire and lava both glow
Sunstone sparkles
Tigers and foxes are regal.
Boldness of the sunset
As the sun falls from the sky
Taking into account all the colors from the day.

Loss

Grief
Is tremendous misery.
Love and loss
Fill our hearts to their fullest
And shatter our hearts to pieces.
Perhaps we are surprised by a loss
Or heartache.
A loved one leaves,
Whether they leave "our" world
Or "the" world
Matters not.
The pain felt can be of the same magnitude.
Left with sadness,
Anger,
Emptiness,
Immense lostness.
Continuing to move onward
Feels like a tragedy
As if I"m not meant to do so
Without my loved one by my side.
The world keeps spinning
Not caring about my ache.
How dare she?
The unfairness of it all
Is not unique.
Yet it feels individualized
Compartmentalized

My own.
Even if we share in it
Your loss is not my loss
It is my own.
Suffering and struggling
Finding a new rhythm
Learning an unfamiliar way
To find comfort and strength.
Stepping forward
Fighting to move on
Growth.
It may hurt less with time
Or it may not.
Or it may just hurt differently
Changing from an intense agony
To a low, dull tingle.
Every instance
Every being
Is different.
This doesn't mean I will forget -
The absence,
The impact,
The sorrow,
The pain.
I carry it with me
As I continue on
Learning from it
Letting it guide me
But not letting it bury me.
I will get through this.

Revolution

I've been referred to as patient (a virtue)
And also stubborn (a downfall).
Both are borne of the same spectrum
Tenacious and strong-willed in there somewhere
too.
I do agree, I am all of the above
But I see no downfall in it.
Why is it if I'm patient with others
It's more of a rewarding trait?
Go easy on them
Show some grace.
That's fair and reasonable
And I don't disagree.
But when I dig my feet in for my own accord,
Resolutely defending a fact
I am cast aside,
Attacked for my doggedness.
No grace for the same steadfastness
Of my own accord.
It is not arrogance
That causes me to persevere and stay true to
myself.
I want others to know what I stand for, sure,
But my tenacity is not selfish.
If I hold my ground for myself,
Patiently listening and quietly contemplating,
Speaking what needs to be spoken,
Know that I will do the same for you too.

Something About the Rain

I've always enjoyed the rain
It evokes relaxation
A slowdown
Pause.
"Take a break," it says
As I watch the gray sky,
Clouds bursting forth,
Droplets running down the window.
It's a perfect moment
To make tea,
Curl up with a good book,
Or even take a nap.
Listening to the showers
Pattering on the roof
The hypnotic thrum.
Methodic.
Cathartic.
This liquid sunshine
Creates a gloomy perception
But I enjoy the grayness,
The darkness
Of the occasion.
Plans may be ruined
Which can be a blessing
In disguise;

Constantly running
Is no way to thrive.
Take a step back
Breathe in the earthiness,
Drops pelting out a rhythm
With impromptu thunder.
A background reminder
To settle in
For a moment of rest
With Mother Nature,
Her soft chorus
That of a lullaby.

Wolves

Clouds drift by
The moon shines bright.
A low, ominous howl begins,
Calling out to each other.
An eeriness takes over the land
As the intensity grows,
Greater numbers increasing the call.
Are there more of them, or
Is that just the echo off the woods
Sounding closer,
Larger?
Prey huddles, trembling -
Condonable, considering the outcry.
Not all who know them,
Love them.
Not all who love them,
Know them.
Brave beasts share the night
Working together to survive.
Amazing creatures,
Family in nature,
Bonded and loyal.
Fierce and protective.
Trusting and faithful
Toward their inner circle.

Intelligent and focused
On the task at hand.
Teamwork to reach achievements,
Yet craving freedom.
Oh, the skills and qualities
That can be learned from a pack
Deserving respect and admiration
As they prowl the night.

Life Lessons

Remember when you were but a child,
And you couldn't do just anything you wanted?
Couldn't go just anywhere you wanted?
Always reliant upon others to take care of you,
To provide you with your needs
And wants.
But you lacked freedom.
Life was hard.
Remember when you were a teenager,
Learning who you were?
Who you wanted to become?
Testing the waters,
Becoming a better version of yourself -
Or in some cases, a worse version.
Pressures around you increasing,
Gauging who you can trust.
Life was tough.
Remember when you were a young adult,
Thrown into the world to survive on your own?
Finally! Freedom!
But it was scary,
All that responsibility.
Still growing, still learning,
And providing for yourself.
Maybe falling in love, maybe not.
Maybe continuing education and training,
maybe not.

Maybe having kids, maybe not.
Regardless of the "maybes"
There can be feelings of inadequacy
When you don't keep up appearances.
Life was so tough.
Remember when you hit middle age
And you were still dealing with all those
"maybes"?
They never go away
But you started to realize that time wasn't on
your side.
Your responsibilities continued to grow in life
Or perhaps they didn't.
Either way, you might think you missed out on
something
Or wonder "what if"?
Replaying scenarios from throughout your life.
So you got that tattoo that you always wanted
Because dammit, life is short.
The younger generation razzed you for going
through a midlife crisis
But if that means caring less about perceptions
And finally following through on a dream
you've had
Then what is so wrong with that?
Life is tough.
Remember when you were in the nursing home
Wondering how time flew by so fast?
So many years gone in a flash.

Suddenly you had all this sage advice
But you grumble because no one listens to you
anyway.
You remember, you didn't listen back then
either.
If only they could see
All that you had seen.
Guide them
But let them make their own mistakes
And forge their own path.
All this experience,
Clearly you knew better than anyone else.
Life was tough.

Life lessons aren't always clear
But we need to open our eyes and pay attention
At all stages of life.
So many things are happening around us
That we tune out
Blindly walking our path
With tunnel vision.
Look up, look around,
It's never too late to pause and take stock.
Learn something new,
Teach someone,
And enjoy the space you occupy.
Life is tough
But we're tougher.

Snowglobe

There is a beauty
In an early morning snowfall
That is incredibly personal.
Waking in the wee hours
To shovel snow in the driveway
Before the neighborhood rises for the day.
Donning snow pants and boots,
Jacket and gloves,
A final deep sigh of resignation
Responsibility reigns for cleanup
Of the undisturbed white fluff.
Slowly, the garage door opens
Revealing the blanket
Encompassing driveways,
Yards,
Roads.
Looking up at the streetlight,
Backdrop of the black night sky,
Plump snowflakes continually drifting to the
ground.
It's like being the object
Inside a snowglobe moments after shaken
When time seems to slow down.
Silence.
All is muted,

Muffled by the cover of insulation.
Not even footfalls make a sound
While imprinting the path.
Feeling like the only person
On the planet
In existence
At that point in time.
Falling snow and exhaling breath
In the cold air
Are the exclusive motions.
Beautiful world.
It's a shame to break the barrier
To strike shovel to pavement
The resounding noise
Seemingly echoing all around.
Reality is the noisiness
Is being muffled the same as before,
It is only the closeness
That makes it intrusive.
These snowglobe instances
Are peaceful one-on-ones
With Old Man Winter
Where we call a brief truce
Enjoyment found
In the simplicity.

Darkness

As nightfall beckons
Trepidation consumes
Not loneliness
But worry.
Not wanting to face
Tomorrow's struggles
And not wanting to return
To yesterday's.
Solace in the night
Without commitments
Or engagements.
Owls hooting
In distant trees
A comfort in their companionship.
Frogs croaking by the marsh
The cacophony an ironic relaxation.
Body fighting to stay awake
For the freeness of the night
Yet wanting to rest
From exhaustion of the day.
Shooting star streaking across the sky
Make a wish!
Blink.
Gone.
Deep breath.

Time to bid the dark adieu
And say goodnight
Succumbing to sleep
Another day done.

Dance Dance Dance

Dance to make yourself happy
Do it when no one is around
In the kitchen
While making dinner
No music required.
Be silly
Enjoy the movement.

Dance when you are glad
Alone or in public
Whichever possesses you
It's contagious
You were warned
Have fun
Take joy in the movement.

Dance when you are frustrated
Let out the aggravation
Fists in the air
Burning off steam
Creating a weariness
Let go
Indulge in the movement.

Dance in the rain

Hop in puddles
Twirl in the mist
Let the water soothe you
Caress you
Get soaked
Relish the movement.

Dance to inspire yourself
Boost your confidence
Be your best champion
Smile at yourself
Kick it up
Get excited
Bask in the movement.

Dance with a partner
Embrace each other
Sway in time
Slow with the music
Share a tender moment
In love
Savor the movement.

Monsters

Monsters under our beds
Or in our closets
Figments of our imagination
Can be the scariest things
Because we don't let ourselves
Believe the truth
Letting stories and thoughts run rampant
Within our minds
Engorging the tales
And the fears
The monsters continue growing
With us as we age
Morphing into larger boogeymen
As the reality of the world
Combines with our imaginations
The known and the unknown
Blurring the lines
Scaring us endlessly
We don't have to live in fear of our monsters
We can stand tall against them
Shine a light on them
Expose them
Make them disappear
They are only as large as we make them

Dear Self

Don't underestimate yourself
Listen to your gut
Believe that you have what it takes
You are beautiful
Take care of yourself
Pray
Stop being so hard on yourself
Ask for help
You are smart
Don't pretend to be something you're not for
someone else -
Be your wonderfully authentic self
Love
Stand tall
Sit up straight
You are worth it
Try new foods
Learn about different cultures
Cry
Read books
Watch movies
Get outside
You are enough
Enjoy someone else's company
Laugh

Go for a bike ride
Play with your dog, or any dog
Put a puzzle together
You are loved
Watch the sunrise
Watch the sunset
Gaze at the stars
Breathe
Buy yourself flowers, don't wait for anyone else
to do it
Be confident in yourself
You are strong
Don't ever forget where you came from
Run
Don't fear the unknown
Or, fear it but move forward anyway
You are brave
Hug someone
Get your hands dirty
Pause
Stop caring so much about what other people
think
Take advice from those who love you
Be present
Help someone else
You have a voice
Smile
I'm sorry it's taken so long to figure out some of
these things

I wish I could go back in time and give you all
of these lines earlier in life
I'm sorry I didn't take care of you better, sooner
Physically
Mentally
But it's never too late
Start now
Keep going
Live.